MUSICAL INSTRUMENTS OF THE WORLD

Strings

Barrie Carson Turner

Illustrated by John See

Belitha Press

First published in the UK in 1998 by
Belitha Press Limited
London House, Great Eastern Wharf,
Parkgate Road, London SW11 4NQ

Editor: Claire Edwards
Series designer: Simeen Karim
Picture researcher: Juliet Duff
Educational consultant: Celia Pardaens

ISBN 1 85561 788 9

Printed in Hong Kong / China

British Library Cataloguing in Publication Data
for this book is available from the British Library.

9 8 7 6 5 4 3 2 1

Picture acknowledgements: Sue Cunningham Photographic: 15;
Eye Ubiquitous: 27; Getty Images: 29; The Hutchison Library: 9, 17,
21, 23, 26; Panos Pictures: 13; Performing Arts Library: 6, 11, 12,
16, 19, 20, 25; Redferns: 4-5, 7, 22; John Walmsley Photo Library: 8.

Contents

Musical

Musical instruments are played in every country of the world. There are thousands of different instruments of all shapes and sizes. They are often grouped into four families: strings, brass, percussion and woodwind.

String instruments sound when their strings vibrate. Percussion instruments are struck (hit), shaken or scraped to make their sound. Brass and woodwind instruments are blown to make their sound.

This book is about the string family. String instruments can be plucked, struck, or bowed. Most have a hollow body, called a soundbox.

instruments

Some soundboxes are simple, others are carved into beautiful shapes. For this book we have chosen 19 string instruments from around the world. There is a picture of each instrument, and a photograph of a performer playing it. On pages 30 and 31 you will find a list of useful words to help you understand more about music.

Double bass

The double bass is the largest and lowest-sounding member of the string family. It has four thick strings. The player pulls a bow across the strings to make them sound. Players often pluck the strings, especially when they play jazz. This adds a bounce to the music. The tallest double bass ever made is almost 5 metres high.

tuning peg

bow

string

fingerboard

sound hole

bridge

spike

Double bass players stand up, or sit on a high stool when they play.

6

Mandolin

tuning peg

fret

The mandolin was first played in Italy about 300 years ago. It is shaped like a pear and has a deep body. Mandolins are often prettily decorated. The metal strings are plucked with a plastic plectrum. Mandolin players play each note quickly, many times, which makes a beautiful shimmering sound.

fingerboard

sound hole

bridge

strings

People often play folk music on the mandolin.

Cello

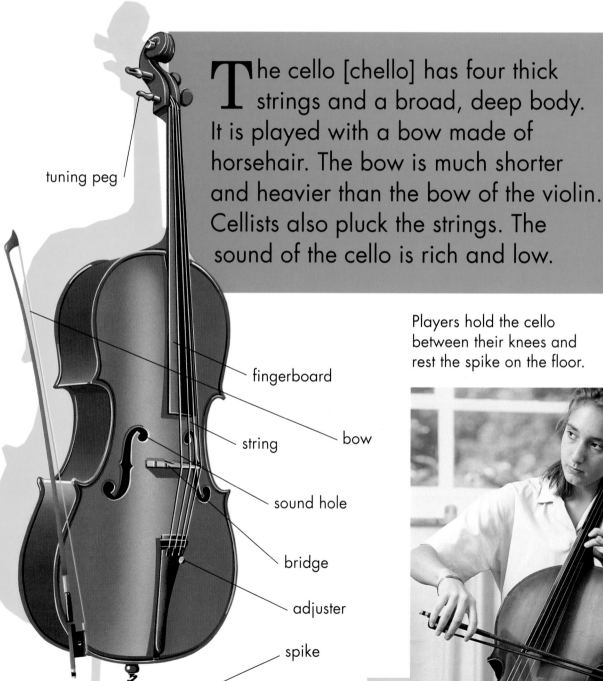

The cello [chello] has four thick strings and a broad, deep body. It is played with a bow made of horsehair. The bow is much shorter and heavier than the bow of the violin. Cellists also pluck the strings. The sound of the cello is rich and low.

tuning peg

fingerboard

string

bow

sound hole

bridge

adjuster

spike

Players hold the cello between their knees and rest the spike on the floor.

8

Moon guitar

The moon guitar has been played in China for more than 1500 years. It is called the moon guitar because of its lovely round shape. It has four strings which are tuned by turning the long pegs. Players use their fingers or a plectrum to pluck the strings.

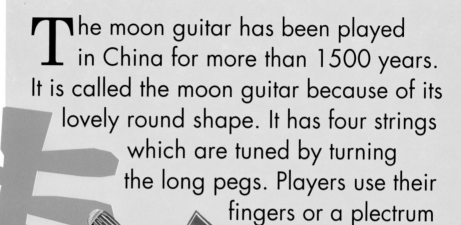

tuning peg

fret

string

bridge

The moon guitar has a quiet, delicate sound. Because of this, it is often used to accompany singers.

Sitar

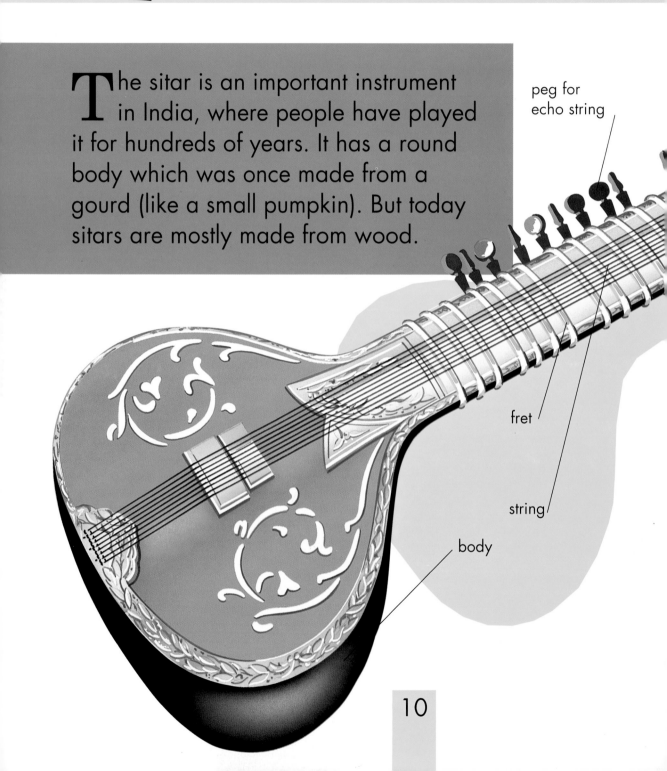

The sitar is an important instrument in India, where people have played it for hundreds of years. It has a round body which was once made from a gourd (like a small pumpkin). But today sitars are mostly made from wood.

peg for echo string

fret

string

body

10

neck

The sitar is plucked with a wire plectrum. The highest sounding string plays the tune. The thin bands of metal along the neck are called frets. The frets can be moved. They are placed in different places for different tunes. The player pulls the string across the fret, which gives the sitar its whining sound.

Sitar players only pluck the strings held by the large pegs. When they do this the strings held by the small pegs make an echo sound.

Banjo

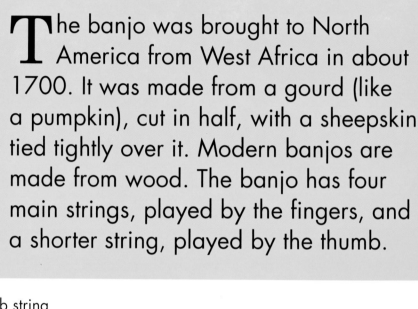

The banjo was brought to North America from West Africa in about 1700. It was made from a gourd (like a pumpkin), cut in half, with a sheepskin tied tightly over it. Modern banjos are made from wood. The banjo has four main strings, played by the fingers, and a shorter string, played by the thumb.

fret

thumb string

fingerboard

belly

string

bridge

Players pluck the strings of the banjo like a guitar, or sometimes brush the strings with the back of their nails.

Ukulele

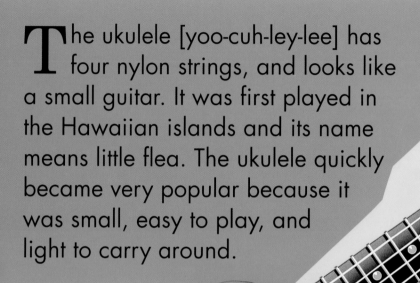

The ukulele [yoo-cuh-ley-lee] has four nylon strings, and looks like a small guitar. It was first played in the Hawaiian islands and its name means little flea. The ukulele quickly became very popular because it was small, easy to play, and light to carry around.

string

fret

fingerboard

sound hole

The ukulele is plucked and strummed like a guitar. It has a bright twanging sound.

13

Cimbalom

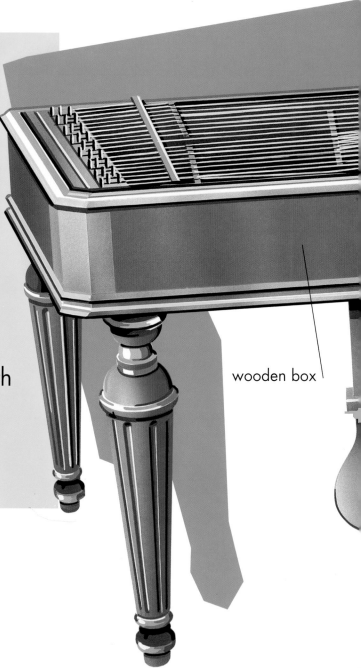

The cimbalom [chim-bal-om] comes from Hungary. It looks like a large wooden box on legs. Inside the box there are many strings. The player taps the strings with thin wooden or wire beaters. The beaters are covered with soft cloth which helps to give the instrument its warm ringing sound.

wooden box

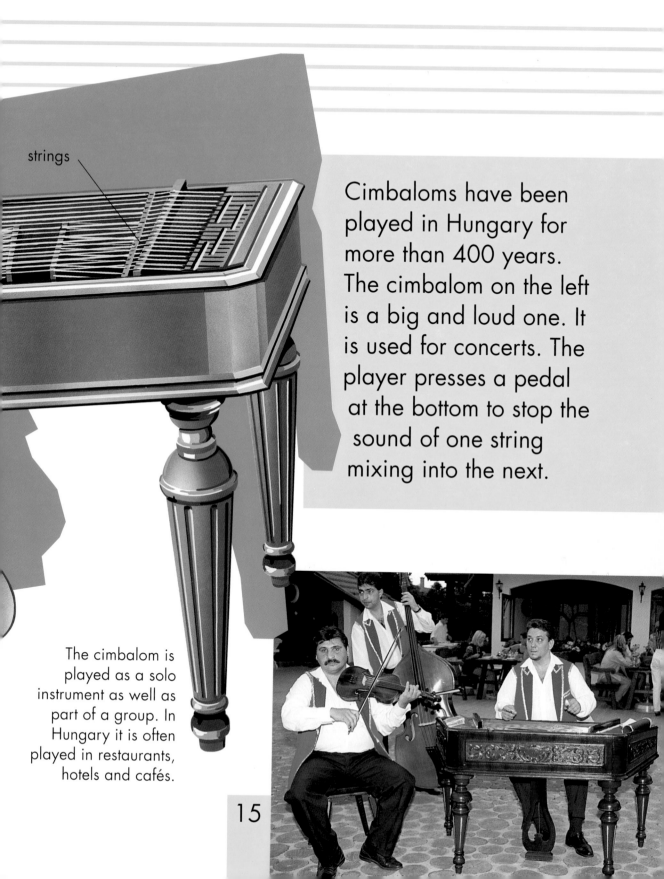

strings

Cimbaloms have been played in Hungary for more than 400 years. The cimbalom on the left is a big and loud one. It is used for concerts. The player presses a pedal at the bottom to stop the sound of one string mixing into the next.

The cimbalom is played as a solo instrument as well as part of a group. In Hungary it is often played in restaurants, hotels and cafés.

15

Violin

The violin has four strings, a curved body and is played with a bow. The bow is made of wood and horsehair. The violinist pulls the hair across the strings to make them sound. Sometimes violinists pluck the strings too. Violin music can sound gentle and sweet, or loud and strong.

tuning peg

fingerboard

string

bow

bridge

sound hole

adjuster

chin rest

Violinists use their fingers to press the strings on to the fingerboard to make different notes.

16

Dulcimer

tuning peg

sound hole

strings

bridge

beaters

soundbox

Dulcimer
(dul-si-ma)
players usually rest
the instrument on their
knees or a table. They tap
the strings with beaters
made of wood or wire.
They also pluck the strings
with their fingers or a
plectrum. The dulcimer has
been played for hundreds
of years in gipsy music
all around Europe.

The player hits the strings gently
with the curved part of the beater
to make a soft ringing sound.

17

Koto

The koto is one of Japan's most famous instruments. It is long and narrow and rests on the ground. Its curved body is made of wood. Once upon a time the strings on a koto were made of silk. Nowadays they are usually made of nylon. Players pluck the strings with plectrums that fit over the thumb and two fingers of the right hand. The plectrums look like small thimbles.

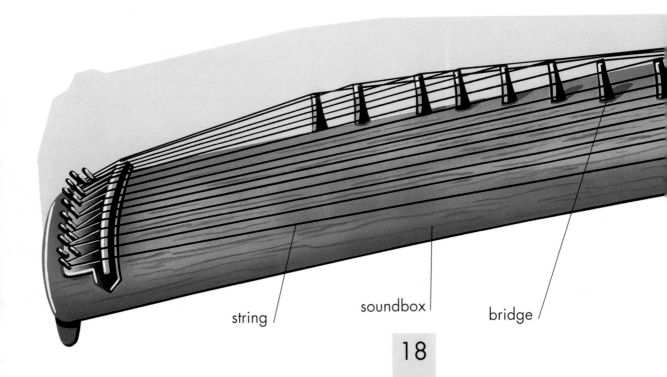

string   soundbox   bridge

In Japan, people often play the koto at home to entertain their family and friends. It can be played as a solo instrument, or to accompany other instruments and singers.

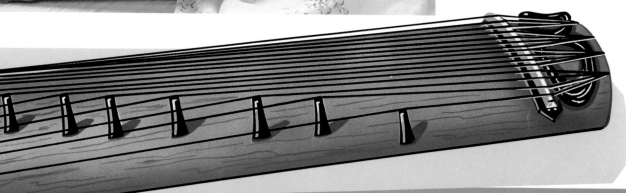

Each string has its own bridge, shaped like the letter Y, but upside down. The bridges hold the strings away from the body of the instrument, which allows them to sound clearly.

Viola

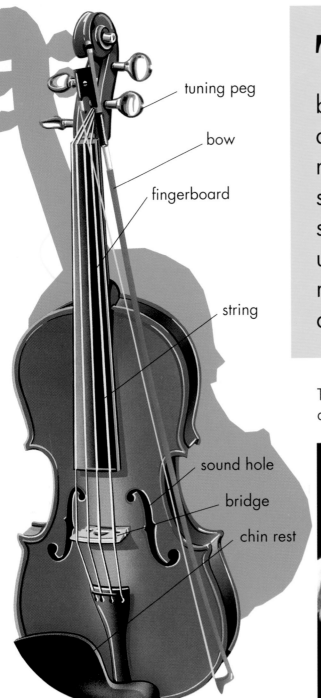

tuning peg

bow

fingerboard

string

sound hole

bridge

chin rest

The viola looks like the violin, but it is a bit bigger. It has four strings and is played with a bow made of horsehair. Players sometimes also pluck the strings. The viola is mainly used in orchestras. Not many people play it as a solo instrument.

The sound of the viola is lower and richer than the violin's sound.

Bandura

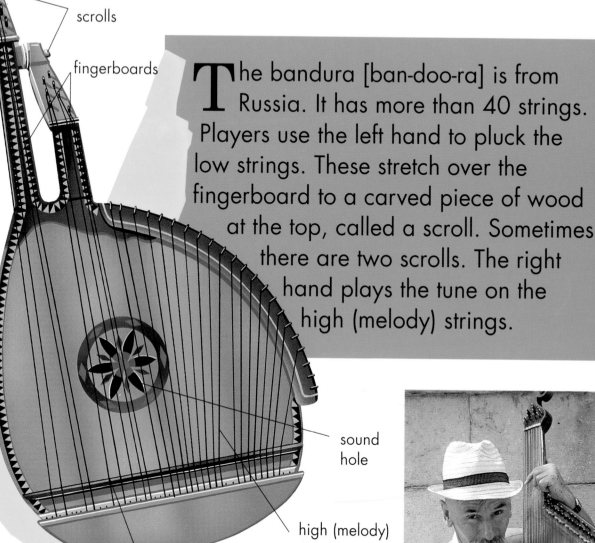

scrolls

fingerboards

The bandura [ban-doo-ra] is from Russia. It has more than 40 strings. Players use the left hand to pluck the low strings. These stretch over the fingerboard to a carved piece of wood at the top, called a scroll. Sometimes there are two scrolls. The right hand plays the tune on the high (melody) strings.

sound hole

high (melody) string

low string

The bandura sounds like a small harp. It is played as a solo instrument and also in groups.

Guitar

The guitar was first played in Spain more than 400 years ago. Today it is used to play pop and classical music. The fingerboard has thin strips of metal called frets, which show guitarists where to put their fingers. They can play single notes, or chords. Guitar strings are plucked or strummed with the fingers, or with a plectrum.

In classical music, guitarists play sitting down, the guitar resting on one leg. Pop musicians usually play standing up.

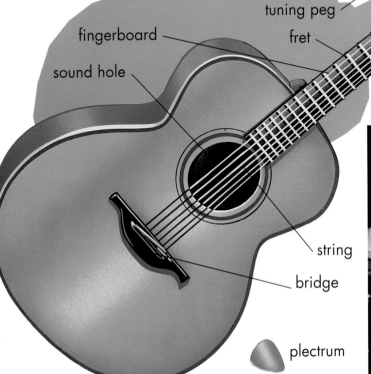

tuning peg

fingerboard

fret

sound hole

string

bridge

plectrum

Musical bow

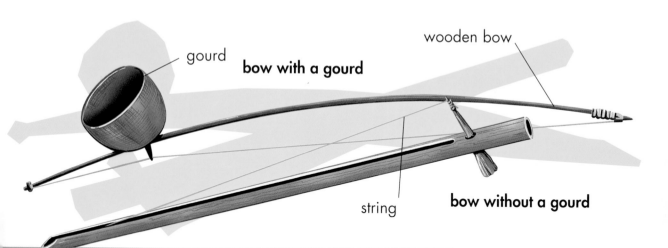

gourd

bow with a gourd

wooden bow

string

bow without a gourd

The musical bow is one of the oldest string instruments. The bow is shaped like a shooting bow. Musicians pluck the string, rub it with a short stick or bow, or even play it with their teeth. Sometimes they fix a hollow gourd, or even a tin can, to the stick, to help make the instrument sound louder.

The musical bow is played in many parts of the world. Musicians sing as they play, or they accompany singers or other instruments.

23

Harp

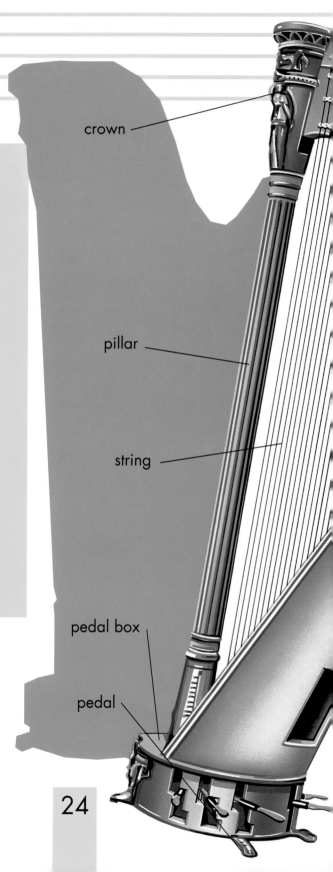

The first harps were played thousands of years ago. Today there are harps of many shapes and sizes all over the world. The orchestral harp is very big and often beautifully decorated. It has 48 strings that stretch from the wavy top edge of the instrument to the wide sloping side. Harpists tilt the harp towards them as they play.

crown

pillar

string

pedal box

pedal

24

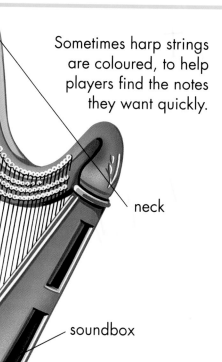

Sometimes harp strings are coloured, to help players find the notes they want quickly.

neck

soundbox

Harpists pluck the strings from both sides. Usually they use their right hand to play the higher (shorter) strings and their left hand to play the low (longer) strings. Players sometimes brush their fingers across the strings to make a beautiful wave of sound. At the base of the harp there are seven pedals. Pressing the pedals makes the strings sound different notes.

Bouzouki

The bouzouki [buh-zoo-ki] is a folk instrument from Greece. It has a very long neck. The eight metal strings are divided into sets of two. Each set of strings plays the same note, and the strings are always played two at a time, in their sets. The bouzouki has metal frets like the guitar.

tuning peg

fret

fingerboard

body

sound hole

bridge

string

Bouzouki players use a plectrum to pluck the metal strings.

26

Balalaika

The Russian balalaika [bal-al-eye-ka] has a body shaped like a triangle, and a flat back. It has three strings. The highest string is made of metal. Players pluck it with their forefinger to play the tune. The other strings are made of nylon. Players pluck them with their thumb to accompany the tune.

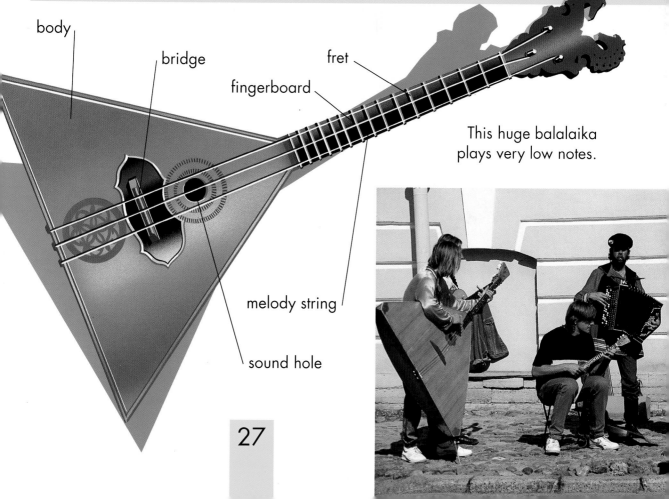

body

bridge

fret

fingerboard

This huge balalaika plays very low notes.

melody string

sound hole

Zither

fret

melody string

sound hole

accompaniment string

The zither comes in many shapes and sizes. It is played resting on a table, or on the player's lap. The five strings on the straight side are used to play the melody. The other strings are used to accompany the melody.

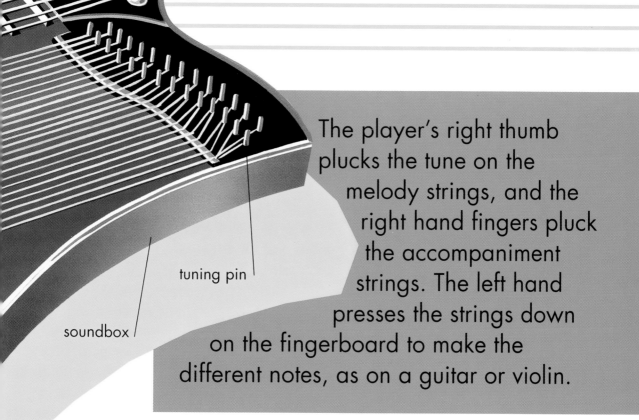

tuning pin

soundbox

The player's right thumb plucks the tune on the melody strings, and the right hand fingers pluck the accompaniment strings. The left hand presses the strings down on the fingerboard to make the different notes, as on a guitar or violin.

Sometimes players shake their left hand as they press down the strings. This makes a wavering sound in the music, which is called vibrato.

Words to

accompaniment Notes that are played along with the tune.

accompany To play music alongside a singer or another player who has the tune.

adjuster A small metal grip that helps to tighten the strings on the violin, viola, cello and double bass.

beaters Sticks of wood or wire used to hit or strike some instruments.

belly The front part of the body of a string instrument.

bow A long piece of wood with horsehair or nylon stretched between the ends. Musicians pull the hair across the strings.

bridge A small piece of wood or other material used to hold the strings away from the body of the instrument so that they sound freely.

chords Groups of notes played together.

concert When players or singers perform in front of an audience.

family (of instruments) Instruments that are similar to each other.

fingerboard A long strip of wood glued to the neck of a string instrument. The player presses the strings against the fingerboard to make different notes.

folk music Popular tunes so old, no one knows who wrote them.

frets Thin strips, usually made of metal, on a fingerboard. They show players where to put their fingers to make notes on an instrument.

jazz A kind of pop music. In jazz, musicians often make up the music at the same time as they play it.

remember

melody A tune.

musician Someone who plays an instrument or sings.

neck The long end-part of a string instrument. The player holds the instrument by the neck with the left hand.

orchestra A large group of musicians playing together.

pedal Any part of an instrument worked by the player's foot.

performer Someone who plays or sings to other people.

plectrum A small piece of plastic or wood used to pluck some string instruments.

pluck To play an instrument by pulling the strings quickly with the fingers, and letting go again.

solo A piece played or sung by one player or singer.

soundbox The hollow body of a string instrument. The soundbox helps to make the instrument louder.

sound hole A round or long hole, or holes, cut into the belly of a string instrument to make it sound better.

strum To pull the fingers across the strings quickly, like a guitarist.

tuning pegs Pegs that can be turned to tighten or loosen the strings until they sound the right note.

vibrate To move up and down very quickly. When a string is bowed or plucked it vibrates.

vibrato A wavering sound in the music made by players shaking their hand as they press down a string.

31

Index